PRINCEWILL LAGANG

Marriage and Mental Health: Supporting Each Other

First published by PRINCEWILL LAGANG 2023

Copyright © 2023 by Princewill Lagang

All rights reserved. No part of this publication may be reproduced, stored or transmitted in any form or by any means, electronic, mechanical, photocopying, recording, scanning, or otherwise without written permission from the publisher. It is illegal to copy this book, post it to a website, or distribute it by any other means without permission.

Princewill Lagang asserts the moral right to be identified as the author of this work.

First edition

This book was professionally typeset on Reedsy.
Find out more at reedsy.com

# Contents

| | | |
|---|---|---|
| 1 | Introduction | 1 |
| 2 | Mental Health Awareness | 4 |
| 3 | The Impact of Mental Health on Marriage | 7 |
| 4 | Open Communication | 10 |
| 5 | Recognizing Signs and Seeking Help | 14 |
| 6 | Navigating Mood Swings and Fluctuations | 17 |
| 7 | Providing Emotional Support | 19 |
| 8 | Balancing Individual and Shared Well-Being | 22 |
| 9 | Coping as a Team | 25 |
| 10 | Self-Care Strategies for Partners | 29 |
| 11 | Professional Help and Therapy | 33 |
| 12 | Cultivating Resilience and Hope | 37 |

# 1

# Introduction

In a world where the complexities of modern life often challenge the foundation of human relationships, this book delves into a crucial yet often overlooked aspect of marital dynamics: the profound interplay between marriage and mental health. As we embark on this journey of exploration, we find ourselves at the crossroads of two fundamental elements of human existence: our need for meaningful connections and our intricate emotional landscapes.

Marriage, a timeless institution that binds two individuals in a sacred and intricate bond, offers a unique vantage point to observe the ebbs and flows of mental well-being. It is within this intimate partnership that our emotional vulnerabilities are both magnified and assuaged, where our deepest fears and desires intertwine with those of our beloved. This book sets out to navigate this delicate terrain, shedding light on the symbiotic relationship between the health of a marriage and the mental wellness of its participants.

At the heart of this exploration lies a recognition of the paramount importance of understanding and supporting each other's mental well-being. Gone are the days when marriage was solely perceived as a union based on practicality or societal norms. In the modern era, we find ourselves in relationships that thrive not just on shared responsibilities, but also on shared emotional experiences. The notion of a partner being a "soulmate" encompasses a deep connection that extends beyond the physical and delves into the realms of mental and emotional resonance.

Yet, as we embrace this paradigm shift, we must also confront the challenges it presents. The pressures of daily life, the strains of work, and the rapid pace of change can all take their toll on our mental equilibrium. Moreover, the emotional closeness inherent in marriage can amplify these challenges, potentially leading to conflicts and misunderstandings. Hence, the need for a comprehensive understanding of the intricacies of mental health within the context of a marriage becomes increasingly imperative.

In the chapters that follow, we will embark on a multidimensional exploration. We will delve into the psychological underpinnings of a healthy marriage, examining how individual mental health influences the collective partnership, and vice versa. We will dissect the role of effective communication, empathy, and vulnerability in nurturing both marital satisfaction and emotional well-being. Drawing upon real-life stories, expert insights, and research findings, we will unravel the tapestry of marital relationships woven with the threads of mental health.

As we embark on this journey, let us remain open to the possibilities that lie ahead. Let us recognize that the challenges we encounter are not insurmountable barriers, but rather opportunities for growth and deeper connection. By undertaking this exploration, we commit ourselves to fostering marriages that are not only strong in their foundation but resilient in the face of adversity. For in the intersection of marriage and mental health, we discover the potential for profound healing, transformative growth, and enduring love.

## INTRODUCTION

Thank you for the opportunity to be part of this journey.

# 2

# Mental Health Awareness

In our endeavor to explore the intricate intersection of marriage and mental health, we must first address a pervasive barrier that has long shrouded these discussions: the stigma surrounding mental health. This chapter embarks on a journey of understanding, where we confront the social norms that have perpetuated silence and misconceptions, while also championing the necessity for mental health awareness within the context of marriage.

Breaking the Silence: Addressing the Stigma

Mental health challenges have historically been veiled in a shroud of silence, relegated to the periphery of conversations, and often held captive by societal stigma. This stigma has led to a culture of shame and secrecy, discouraging individuals from seeking the help they deserve. It is time to peel back the layers of misunderstanding and ignorance that have fueled this stigma.

Understanding that mental health is as vital as physical health is crucial in dismantling this stigma. Just as we care for our bodies, nurturing our minds is equally essential. By encouraging open dialogues, challenging stereotypes, and sharing personal stories, we can actively counteract the stigma and create a safe space where individuals feel empowered to seek assistance when needed.

Mental Health Challenges in Relationships

Marriage, as a union of emotional intimacy, exposes partners to each other's emotional landscapes in ways that other relationships may not. Consequently, mental health challenges can significantly impact the dynamics of a marriage. From anxiety and depression to more complex conditions, the prevalence of mental health issues in relationships is undeniable.

In fact, studies have shown that partners of individuals with mental health challenges often experience their own emotional strains, ranging from feelings of helplessness to burnout. Furthermore, the strain of supporting a partner through such difficulties can potentially lead to communication breakdowns and emotional distancing, further exacerbating the challenges faced by both individuals.

The Need for Mental Health Awareness in Marital Context

Navigating mental health challenges within a marriage necessitates a deep well of empathy, understanding, and patience. This is where mental health awareness steps in as a crucial guiding light. By equipping ourselves with knowledge about various mental health conditions, their symptoms, and potential treatments, we can foster a more compassionate and informed environment within our marriages.

Through this awareness, we can learn to recognize when a partner may be struggling and provide a supportive space for them to share their experiences. Communication becomes a bridge, allowing partners to openly discuss their emotional states, fears, and needs. It is through these conversations that the bonds of trust are strengthened and the foundation of a resilient marriage is built.

In the chapters ahead, we will delve deeper into specific mental health challenges, offering insights and strategies for navigating them within the context of a marriage. By shedding light on these often complex topics, we aim to empower couples to face challenges head-on, fostering relationships that are characterized by compassion, resilience, and a shared commitment to emotional well-being.

Thank you for accompanying us on this journey of understanding and growth. Together, we will transcend the limitations of stigma and forge a path toward mental health awareness and support within the realm of marriage.

# 3

# The Impact of Mental Health on Marriage

As we delve deeper into the intricate relationship between marriage and mental health, this chapter serves as a bridge connecting theory with lived experience. We explore the profound impact that mental health issues can have on the dynamics of a marriage, unraveling the intricate threads that tie emotional well-being to the very fabric of partnership.

The Ripple Effect of Mental Health Challenges

Mental health issues within a marriage are akin to a stone cast into a still pond, creating ripples that extend far beyond the initial impact. One partner's emotional struggles can reverberate through the relationship, affecting communication, understanding, and intimacy. It is crucial to recognize that the challenges faced by one partner are, in essence, shared challenges that require a united approach.

Communication Challenges

Effective communication is the bedrock of any healthy relationship, and marriage is no exception. However, mental health challenges can introduce unique hurdles to this essential aspect of connection. Partners may struggle to articulate their emotions, leading to misunderstandings or frustration. In some cases, withdrawal and silence can become prevalent, deepening the emotional chasm between partners.

In the face of such challenges, cultivating empathetic communication becomes paramount. Active listening, patience, and the willingness to create a safe space for open dialogue can help partners bridge the gap created by mental health issues. By approaching conversations with compassion and without judgment, couples can create an environment where both partners feel heard and understood.

Emotional Support and Empathy

Marriage is often described as a partnership where two individuals support each other through life's ups and downs. However, when mental health issues arise, providing effective emotional support can become more complex. Partners may grapple with their own feelings of helplessness, uncertainty about how to provide the right support, or even a fear of exacerbating the situation.

Empathy, a cornerstone of emotional connection, plays a crucial role in navigating this terrain. Partners who actively strive to understand each other's emotional experiences can offer the reassurance and validation needed to foster a sense of security. Expressing love, patience, and a willingness to learn about the specific challenges associated with a particular mental health condition can create a strong foundation for emotional support.

Impact on Intimacy

Intimacy, both physical and emotional, is a cherished aspect of marriage.

However, mental health challenges can cast a shadow over this intimate space. Feelings of anxiety, depression, or even medication side effects can influence one's capacity for connection. It is vital to understand that shifts in intimacy are not indicative of a lack of love, but rather a reflection of the complex interplay between mental health and emotional bonds.

Navigating these challenges requires a delicate balance of patience and adaptability. Partners can work together to explore new ways of connecting, communicate openly about their needs and boundaries, and seek professional guidance when necessary. By approaching intimacy with understanding and flexibility, couples can nurture a sense of closeness that transcends the barriers posed by mental health challenges.

In the chapters that follow, we will delve into specific mental health conditions and explore strategies for managing their impact on marriage. By embracing these insights, couples can transform challenges into opportunities for growth, deepening their bond and cultivating a partnership that thrives in the face of adversity.

Thank you for your dedication to understanding the intricate dance between mental health and marriage. Together, we will uncover pathways to resilience and connection that are anchored in compassion and shared commitment.

# 4

# Open Communication

Within the landscape of marriage and mental health, open communication stands as a beacon of hope and healing. In this chapter, we explore the transformative power of candid dialogue about mental health, highlighting its pivotal role in fostering understanding, empathy, and resilience within the partnership.

The Foundation of Understanding: Importance of Open Communication

In a marriage where mental health is an integral aspect of the shared journey, open communication becomes an indispensable cornerstone. Transparent conversations serve as a bridge between partners' emotional worlds, enabling them to traverse the intricate terrain of mental health challenges together. By laying bare their thoughts, fears, and aspirations, partners create a space where vulnerability is met with empathy and support.

Furthermore, open communication shatters the walls of silence that stigma has erected. By discussing mental health with honesty and sincerity, couples contribute to the dismantling of misconceptions and pave the way for a society that acknowledges and respects the validity of emotional struggles.

Creating a Safe Haven for Sharing

The process of opening up about mental health requires a nurturing environment where partners can feel safe, heard, and valued. Establishing such a safe haven is a joint effort that requires mutual commitment and care.

1. Active Listening: Listening attentively without interrupting or judging lays the foundation for meaningful conversations. When one partner speaks, the other listens with undivided attention, allowing the speaker to express their thoughts and emotions fully.

2. Nonjudgmental Attitude: Creating a space free from judgment encourages partners to share without fear of criticism. By suspending assumptions and opinions, both partners demonstrate their dedication to understanding and acceptance.

3. Empathetic Responses: Responding with empathy and compassion validates the speaker's feelings and experiences. Acknowledging emotions with phrases like "I can understand how you feel" or "That sounds really tough" reinforces emotional connection.

4. Scheduled Check-ins: Designating specific times for check-ins about mental health fosters consistency and predictability. These conversations can be a regular part of the partnership, helping both partners feel that their emotional well-being is a priority.

5. Setting Boundaries: Establishing boundaries around when and how to approach mental health discussions prevents overwhelm. Partners can decide on a code or signal that indicates when one of them is ready to engage in such a conversation.

6. Respect for Differences: Partners may have differing coping mechanisms and communication styles. Respecting these differences and being patient with each other's pace of opening up is essential.

Strategies for Effective Communication

1. Use "I" Statements: Express feelings and concerns using "I" statements, such as "I feel" or "I think." This shifts the focus to personal experiences and avoids sounding accusatory.

2. Avoid Blame: Frame discussions in a way that avoids assigning blame for emotional struggles. Focus on sharing experiences rather than attributing responsibility.

3. Be Mindful of Timing: Choose a time when both partners are relatively calm and receptive to engage in deeper conversations. Avoid discussing sensitive topics during moments of stress or tension.

4. Practice Patience: Some partners may need time to articulate their feelings. Avoid rushing or pressuring each other to share immediately.

5. Seek Professional Support: If communication becomes consistently challenging, seeking the guidance of a mental health professional or couples therapist can provide tools and techniques to enhance communication skills.

In the chapters ahead, we will delve into specific strategies for addressing different mental health challenges through open communication. By embracing the transformative power of sharing, listening, and understanding, partners can create a marriage that thrives on the strength of their emotional connection.

Thank you for your commitment to nurturing a partnership built on openness and empathy. Together, we embark on a journey of shared growth and emotional well-being.

# 5

# Recognizing Signs and Seeking Help

Within the complex tapestry of marriage, the threads of mental health are interwoven in intricate ways. This chapter focuses on the vital task of recognizing signs of mental health struggles in a partner and navigating the journey of seeking professional help together. By honing the skills to identify and address these challenges, couples lay the foundation for a resilient and supportive partnership.

Understanding the Signs: A Compassionate Approach

Recognizing signs of mental health struggles requires a blend of attentiveness, empathy, and knowledge. Partners are uniquely positioned to observe changes in behavior, mood, and emotions. By approaching this task with a compassionate mindset, they can create an environment where support and understanding flourish.

Subtle Changes: Mental health challenges often manifest as subtle shifts in behavior. Partners may notice alterations in sleep patterns, appetite, or energy levels. Changes in interests, hobbies, or social interactions may also signal emotional distress.

Mood Fluctuations: Rapid mood swings, unexplained irritability, or prolonged periods of sadness are potential indicators of underlying mental health struggles. Partners should be attuned to changes that are uncharacteristic of their loved ones.

Withdrawal: A partner who once enjoyed social interactions or shared activities might start withdrawing from them. They may exhibit a reluctance to engage in conversations or spend time together.

Seeking Professional Help: A Shared Endeavor

When signs of mental health challenges emerge, seeking professional help is a pivotal step. However, this journey is not one that the affected partner should embark upon alone. The process of reaching out for support is a shared endeavor that reinforces the strength of the partnership.

Initiating the Conversation: Approach the topic with empathy and concern. Express that you've noticed changes and are genuinely interested in understanding their experiences. Highlight the idea of seeking help together as an act of partnership, emphasizing that you are there to support them every step of the way.

Researching Professionals: Collaborate in researching mental health professionals who specialize in the specific challenges being faced. Discuss different treatment options, such as therapy, counseling, or medication, to understand what aligns best with their needs.

Accompanying to Appointments: Offer to accompany your partner to appointments, especially during the initial stages. This gesture can provide emotional support and demonstrate your commitment to their well-being.

Being an Active Participant: Attend therapy sessions or couples counseling together, if appropriate. Actively engage in the process, listen attentively, and contribute to the development of coping strategies.

Creating a Supportive Environment

In the journey of seeking help, partners can play a crucial role in creating a supportive environment that nurtures healing and growth.

Encouragement and Validation: Express pride in your partner's courage to seek help and validate their experiences. Emphasize that their well-being matters deeply to you.

Patience and Understanding: Understand that the process of seeking help is not linear. Progress may be slow, and setbacks can occur. Approach these moments with patience and understanding.

Shared Commitment: Mental health challenges affect both partners, and the journey to healing is a shared one. By standing together, you strengthen your bond and create a space where challenges can be faced as a united front.

In the chapters ahead, we will explore specific mental health conditions and their impact on marriage. By recognizing signs and embracing the path of seeking help, couples pave the way for a partnership that flourishes even in the face of adversity.

Thank you for your dedication to fostering an environment of understanding, empathy, and shared growth. Through recognition, support, and collaboration, couples can navigate the challenges of mental health with strength and resilience.

# 6

# Navigating Mood Swings and Fluctuations

Within the landscape of marriage, the ebb and flow of emotional tides is a natural occurrence. This chapter delves into the complexities of mood swings and emotional fluctuations, offering insights into strategies that partners can employ to navigate these challenging moments with grace, patience, and understanding.

Understanding the Dynamics: Embracing Emotional Complexity

Mood swings and emotional fluctuations are part and parcel of the human experience, influenced by a multitude of factors, including stress, hormonal changes, and external events. In the context of marriage, these fluctuations take on a unique dimension, where partners' emotional states are intricately intertwined.

Impact on Communication: Mood swings can lead to unpredictable shifts in emotional availability. Partners may oscillate between moments of connection and periods of withdrawal, creating a sense of uncertainty within the relationship.

Navigating Conflict: Fluctuating emotions can influence how partners engage in conflicts. A partner who is already emotionally overwhelmed might react more intensely or retreat during disagreements.

Strategies for Navigating Mood Swings and Fluctuations

1. Practice Active Listening: During moments of mood swings, be an attentive listener. Allow your partner to express their emotions without judgment, creating a space where they feel validated and heard.

2. Empathetic Responses: Respond to mood swings with empathy. Validate your partner's feelings by expressing understanding

# 7

# Providing Emotional Support

In the intricate dance of marriage and mental health, emotional support serves as a cornerstone of connection and resilience. This chapter delves into the art of offering unwavering emotional support to one another, exploring the ways in which partners can create a safe and nurturing environment where both can thrive.

The Pillars of Emotional Support: Nurturing Connection

Emotional support is a testament to the strength of a partnership, solidifying the bond between partners as they navigate the ebbs and flows of life. This support goes beyond mere words; it is a deliberate effort to understand, validate, and stand by one another in times of need.

Active Listening: The gift of undivided attention is a powerful form of support. When your partner speaks, listen attentively without interruption, demonstrating that their feelings and experiences are important to you.

Validation: Validating your partner's emotions fosters a sense of acceptance. Acknowledge their feelings and experiences as legitimate, even if you may not fully comprehend their perspective.

Creating a Safe Space: Establish an environment where your partner feels secure in expressing their thoughts and emotions without fear of judgment. Openness and nonjudgmental acceptance lay the foundation for honest communication.

Offering Reassurance: During challenging times, express your commitment to stand by your partner's side. Reassure them that you are there to support and share the burden of their struggles.

Empathy: Put yourself in your partner's shoes and attempt to understand their emotional experiences. Empathy fosters a deeper connection and shows that you are invested in their well-being.

Supporting Emotional Expression: Strategies for Partners

1. Validate Emotions: Instead of dismissing or minimizing your partner's feelings, validate their experiences by saying, "It's okay to feel this way."

2. Ask Open-Ended Questions: Encourage open communication by asking questions that invite deeper discussion, such as "How are you feeling?" or "Is there something you'd like to talk about?"

3. Reflective Listening: Repeat back what your partner says to show that you are actively engaged in the conversation and understand their point of view.

4. Express Empathy: Show empathy by saying, "I can imagine how that must feel" or "I'm here for you."

5. Offer Physical Comfort: Physical touch, such as holding hands or offering

a hug, can provide comfort and reassurance.

6. Normalize Feelings: Remind your partner that it's okay to experience a range of emotions and that you're there to support them through it all.

Mutual Exchange of Support

Emotional support is a two-way street in a marriage. Both partners benefit from the compassion, understanding, and validation that come with mutual emotional support. The journey becomes a shared endeavor, and the partnership grows stronger as a result.

In the chapters that follow, we will explore further strategies for addressing specific mental health challenges within the context of a marriage. By cultivating a foundation of emotional support, couples lay the groundwork for a partnership that thrives on empathy, understanding, and shared growth.

Thank you for your dedication to nurturing emotional well-being within your marriage. Through the practice of emotional support, partners forge a connection that can weather any storm.

# 8

# Balancing Individual and Shared Well-Being

In the intricate tapestry of marriage, the delicate art of balancing individual mental health with the well-being of the partnership takes center stage. This chapter explores the dynamic interplay between personal well-being and collective happiness, offering insights into fostering a harmonious equilibrium that supports both partners' growth.

Embracing Individual Well-Being: A Foundation for Partnership

A solid partnership is built upon the strength of two individuals who bring their unique qualities, dreams, and challenges. Prioritizing individual well-being contributes to the vitality of the partnership as a whole.

Self-Care: Encourage one another to engage in self-care activities that nourish mental, emotional, and physical well-being. Recognize that a happier, healthier individual is better equipped to contribute positively to the relationship.

Boundaries: Respect each other's need for personal space and time. Creating healthy boundaries ensures that partners have the freedom to pursue their interests and recharge, fostering a sense of autonomy.

Open Communication: Discuss individual goals, aspirations, and challenges. When partners are aware of each other's personal journeys, they can provide the necessary support and encouragement.

Nurturing Collective Wellness: The Power of Partnership

A thriving partnership requires active attention to the shared well-being of both partners. By investing in collective happiness, partners strengthen their emotional connection and create a foundation for resilience.

Shared Experiences: Engage in activities that bring joy to both partners. Shared experiences create positive memories and foster emotional bonds.

Collaborative Problem-Solving: Approach challenges as a team, working together to find solutions that benefit both individuals and the partnership.

Respecting Differences: Celebrate each other's unique strengths, perspectives, and needs. Acknowledge that differences contribute to the richness of the partnership.

Strategies for Achieving Balance

1. Regular Check-Ins: Schedule regular check-ins where both partners discuss their individual well-being and any concerns. This ensures that both voices are heard and valued.

2. Mindful Communication: Approach conversations about personal

and collective well-being with mindfulness and sensitivity. Avoid making assumptions and be open to each other's feelings.

3. Shared Goals: Identify shared goals that contribute to both individual and collective well-being. This could include setting aside time for activities you both enjoy or cultivating habits that nurture emotional connection.

4. Seeking Professional Guidance: If finding balance becomes challenging, consider seeking the guidance of a couples therapist or counselor. Professional support can provide tools and techniques for maintaining equilibrium.

5. Regular Reflection: Individually and together, take time to reflect on your emotional states and the state of your partnership. This practice promotes self-awareness and helps identify areas that need attention.

A Harmonious Dance of Well-Being

Balancing individual and shared well-being requires intention, effort, and a deep understanding of each other's needs. By honoring the unique journey of each partner while nurturing the collective partnership, couples create a harmonious dance that thrives on mutual growth and emotional connection.

In the chapters ahead, we will continue to explore strategies for addressing specific mental health challenges within the context of a marriage. By embracing the delicate balance between personal and shared well-being, partners foster a partnership that flourishes on a foundation of empathy, support, and harmony.

Thank you for your commitment to cultivating a marriage that honors both individual uniqueness and shared connection. Through this balance, couples unlock the potential for enduring love and resilience.

# 9

# Coping as a Team

In the intricate dance of marriage and mental health, the power of partnership shines brightest when couples face mental health challenges as a united team. This chapter delves into the strategies that partners can employ to navigate the journey of coping together, drawing upon problem-solving techniques, stress reduction methods, and the practice of self-care.

Facing Challenges Hand in Hand: The Strength of Unity

Coping with mental health challenges as a team amplifies the impact of support and resilience. The combined efforts of both partners create a safe space for understanding, growth, and healing.

Shared Problem-Solving: Approach challenges collaboratively. Brainstorm solutions together and consider each other's perspectives to find approaches that work for both partners.

Divide and Conquer: Assign tasks and responsibilities based on each partner's strengths. Dividing responsibilities eases the burden and promotes a sense of shared effort.

Establishing Rituals: Create routines that promote emotional well-being. Rituals like daily check-ins or weekly self-care activities provide consistency and stability.

Techniques for Coping Together

1. Stress Reduction Techniques: Explore stress-reduction techniques as a couple. This could include practicing mindfulness, deep breathing, or engaging in relaxing activities together.

2. Problem-Solving Discussions: When challenges arise, engage in open discussions about potential solutions. Focus on the problem, not on blaming each other, and work collaboratively to find strategies.

3. Team-Based Self-Care: Encourage and participate in each other's self-care routines. This could involve taking walks together, practicing meditation, or simply spending quality time in each other's company.

4. Creating a Relaxing Environment: Design spaces in your home that promote relaxation and tranquility. A comfortable corner for reading, a calming playlist, or soothing scents can contribute to a soothing environment.

5. Quality Time: Dedicate quality time to each other without the pressures of discussing challenges. Engage in activities that bring joy and laughter, fostering emotional connection.

The Power of Self-Care in Partnership

Self-care is not an individual endeavor; it's a practice that can be shared and enhanced within a partnership. Partners who prioritize their own well-being contribute to the strength of the relationship.

Encouraging Self-Care: Support your partner's self-care practices. Encourage them to engage in activities that promote their emotional and mental well-being.

Team-Based Self-Care: Identify self-care practices that can be enjoyed as a team. Whether it's cooking a healthy meal together, going for a nature walk, or practicing a relaxing hobby, the shared experience enhances the benefits.

Balancing Responsibilities: Distribute household and personal responsibilities to create space for self-care activities. Partners can alternate tasks to ensure that both have time for rejuvenation.

Reflection and Growth as a Team

Coping as a team requires ongoing reflection and growth. As partners navigate mental health challenges together, they learn, adapt, and strengthen their bond.

Regular Check-Ins: Schedule regular check-ins to discuss coping strategies, what's working, and what needs adjustment. Use these moments as opportunities for open communication and shared problem-solving.

Adapting and Evolving: Understand that coping strategies may need to evolve over time. Be open to trying new techniques and making adjustments based on the changing nature of challenges.

In the chapters that follow, we will continue to explore specific mental health conditions and strategies for navigating them within the context of a marriage. By embracing coping as a team, partners create a partnership fortified with empathy, support, and a shared commitment to emotional well-being.

Thank you for your dedication to cultivating a relationship that thrives on unity, strength, and the power of mutual coping. Through teamwork, partners forge a path to enduring love and resilience.

# 10

# Self-Care Strategies for Partners

Within the intricate tapestry of marriage and mental health, the importance of self-care for partners becomes paramount. This chapter explores the delicate art of maintaining one's own mental well-being while providing steadfast support to a partner facing challenges. By embracing self-care routines and establishing healthy boundaries, partners ensure they have the emotional reserves needed to nurture the relationship.

Navigating the Dual Role: Self-Care and Support

Being a source of support for a partner while prioritizing one's own well-being may seem challenging, but it's an essential balance that contributes to the health of both individuals and the partnership.

Understanding Personal Needs: Recognize that your well-being is equally important. Prioritizing your mental health empowers you to provide effective support.

The Power of Self-Care: Engaging in self-care routines isn't selfish; it's a means of maintaining your emotional equilibrium and capacity to support your partner.

Mindful Boundaries: Setting healthy boundaries helps prevent emotional exhaustion. Clearly define the times when you need to focus on your own well-being.

Self-Care Routines: Nurturing Your Mental Health

1. Daily Check-Ins: Set aside a few moments each day to check in with yourself. Reflect on your emotions, needs, and any stressors you may be experiencing.

2. Physical Well-Being: Prioritize physical health through regular exercise, a balanced diet, and sufficient sleep. Physical well-being contributes to emotional resilience.

3. Mindfulness and Meditation: Engage in mindfulness practices and meditation to cultivate a sense of calm and presence. These practices enhance your ability to manage stress.

4. Engaging Hobbies: Dedicate time to hobbies or activities that bring you joy and fulfillment. Nurturing your interests contributes to your overall happiness.

5. Social Connection: Maintain social connections outside the partnership. Spending time with friends and family offers additional avenues of emotional support.

Establishing Healthy Boundaries: Nurturing Your Emotional Space

Healthy boundaries protect your mental well-being while preserving your capacity to support your partner effectively.

Communication: Openly discuss your needs and boundaries with your partner. Ensure that both of you are aware of each other's emotional limits.

Scheduled Breaks: Designate times when you focus on self-care without distractions. Inform your partner about these times, ensuring they understand and respect them.

Limiting Absorption: While providing support, remember that you cannot absorb or fix your partner's emotions. Encourage them to seek professional help when needed.

Seeking External Support: The Strength of Community

1. Therapeutic Support: Consider individual therapy or counseling to navigate your own emotions and challenges. A mental health professional can offer personalized guidance.

2. Supportive Network: Surround yourself with a network of friends, family, or support groups who can offer understanding and encouragement.

3. Respite Care: If the situation requires, consider enlisting the help of trusted friends or family members to provide temporary support, allowing you time to recharge.

Reflection and Growth as an Individual and Partner

Balancing self-care with support for your partner is an ongoing journey that requires reflection, adaptability, and a commitment to your own well-being.

Regular Reflection: Regularly assess your own emotional state and the impact of your coping strategies. Make adjustments as needed to maintain a healthy equilibrium.

Open Communication: Continuously communicate with your partner about your own well-being, your boundaries, and your efforts to support them effectively.

In the chapters that follow, we will delve into specific mental health challenges and explore strategies for addressing them within the context of a marriage. By embracing self-care, setting healthy boundaries, and seeking external support when necessary, partners pave the way for a partnership that thrives on empathy, understanding, and mutual growth.

Thank you for your dedication to nurturing your own well-being while supporting your partner. Through this balance, partners foster a partnership that endures challenges and celebrates shared emotional well-being.

# 11

# Professional Help and Therapy

In the intricate interplay of marriage and mental health, the decision to seek professional therapy can be a transformative step toward growth and healing. This chapter delves into the myriad benefits of couples therapy, highlighting its pivotal role in enhancing communication, coping skills, and fostering emotional well-being within the partnership.

Recognizing the Value of Couples Therapy: A Shared Journey

Couples therapy is not an admission of failure but a testament to a partnership's commitment to growth and emotional well-being. This journey is an investment in the strength of the relationship and the individual well-being of both partners.

Neutral Ground: Therapy provides a safe and neutral environment where both partners can openly express their thoughts and emotions without fear of judgment.

Communication Enhancement: Couples therapy equips partners with effective communication tools, enabling them to express themselves clearly and listen actively.

Conflict Resolution: A therapist guides couples in resolving conflicts and disagreements in healthy and productive ways, preventing harmful patterns from escalating.

Fostering Empathy: Therapy encourages partners to see situations from each other's perspectives, fostering a deeper sense of empathy and understanding.

Coping Skills Development: Therapists offer strategies for managing stress, navigating challenges, and supporting each other through emotional struggles.

Improving Emotional Intimacy: By addressing emotional barriers and fostering a sense of vulnerability, therapy enhances emotional intimacy and connection.

Navigating the Therapeutic Process: A Unified Approach

As partners embark on the therapeutic journey, they do so as a united team. Together, they create an environment where open communication, mutual respect, and shared growth thrive.

Selecting the Right Therapist: Research and choose a therapist who specializes in couples therapy and aligns with both partners' needs and values.

Establishing Goals: Define your goals for therapy, whether it's improving communication, resolving conflicts, or managing specific mental health challenges.

Attending Regular Sessions: Consistency is key. Attend therapy sessions as scheduled, allowing time for insights and strategies to take root.

Active Participation: Engage fully in therapy sessions. Be open to sharing your thoughts, feelings, and experiences to maximize the benefits.

Translating Learning to Daily Life: Apply the techniques learned in therapy to real-life situations. Regularly practice communication and coping skills outside of therapy sessions.

Creating a Supportive Post-Therapy Environment

As partners progress through therapy, the insights and skills acquired continue to shape the partnership's trajectory.

Continued Open Communication: Maintain the practice of open, nonjudgmental communication that was cultivated during therapy.

Conflict Resolution: Utilize the conflict resolution techniques learned in therapy to address challenges in a healthy and productive manner.

Regular Check-Ins: Schedule regular check-ins to discuss how the skills learned in therapy are being applied and adapted in real-life situations.

Supporting Each Other's Growth: Recognize that personal growth is an ongoing journey. Continue to support each other's individual well-being and the partnership's collective health.

In the chapters ahead, we will explore specific mental health challenges and strategies for addressing them within the context of a marriage. By embracing the transformative potential of therapy, partners foster a partnership that thrives on understanding, communication, and mutual support.

Thank you for your dedication to nurturing the health of your relationship through therapy. Through this collaborative journey, partners pave the way for a resilient, thriving partnership that navigates challenges with strength and grace.

# 12

# Cultivating Resilience and Hope

As we near the culmination of this exploration into the intertwining realms of marriage and mental health, it's essential to reflect on the journey that partners have undertaken together. This chapter encapsulates the key takeaways from our exploration and offers guidance on fostering a resilient partnership that thrives on understanding, empathy, and hope.

Reflecting on the Journey: Embracing Growth

The journey of supporting each other's mental health is a testament to the strength of your partnership. Each step taken, every conversation had, and every challenge faced has contributed to the growth and evolution of your relationship.

Acknowledging Progress: Take a moment to recognize how far you've come in understanding, supporting, and empathizing with each other's mental well-being.

Communication as a Lifeline: The foundation of your journey has been open and honest communication. Reflect on the positive impact it has had on your emotional connection.

Fostering Resilience: Recognize the resilience you've cultivated as individuals and as a team. Challenges have been met with strength and adaptability.

Key Takeaways: Lessons to Cherish

1. Empathy Nurtures Connection: The power of empathy cannot be overstated. By actively striving to understand each other's emotions, you've deepened your emotional bond.

2. Communication Is a Lifeline: Open and nonjudgmental communication has been the backbone of your support system, bridging emotional gaps and fostering unity.

3. Balancing Individual and Shared Well-Being: The harmony between prioritizing individual mental health and nurturing the partnership is vital for long-term growth.

4. Seeking Professional Help Is a Sign of Strength: By embracing therapy, you've demonstrated your commitment to growth, healing, and the strength of your relationship.

Guidance for a Resilient Partnership: Nurturing Hope

As you continue your journey, here are some guiding principles to uphold the resilience and hope that have brought you this far:

Never Stop Learning: Commit to lifelong learning about each other's emotional landscapes. Your relationship is a dynamic entity that evolves with time.

Celebrate Growth: Acknowledge and celebrate the growth you experience individually and as partners. Celebrate your victories, no matter how small.

Practice Patience: Mental health challenges are not linear. Be patient with yourselves and each other as you navigate the ups and downs.

Maintain Rituals: Continue engaging in rituals and activities that foster connection and emotional well-being. These routines nourish your partnership.

Stay Curious: Approach each other with a sense of curiosity, eager to understand and support each other's emotional experiences.

Remember Your Strength: During challenging times, remind yourselves of the strength you've exhibited as a couple. Lean on that strength to face new challenges.

Cultivating Hope: Nurture a sense of hope by focusing on the progress you've made and the love that underpins your partnership.

Embracing the Journey Ahead

In closing, remember that your journey as partners is ongoing. The chapters that lie ahead are yet to be written, filled with new experiences, challenges, and triumphs.

Thank you for your dedication to nurturing a partnership that thrives on understanding, empathy, and mutual growth. Through the cultivation of resilience and hope, partners forge a path to enduring love and a future filled with shared emotional well-being.

Conclusion: Nurturing Love and Mental Well-Being

In the tapestry of marriage, the threads of mental well-being are woven intricately, creating a partnership that is both resilient and vibrant. Throughout this journey, we've delved into the profound intersection of mental health and relationships, exploring the ways in which open communication, empathy, and mutual support are the cornerstones of a thriving partnership.

A Foundation of Understanding: We've uncovered the significance of understanding mental health challenges and breaking free from the shackles of stigma. By recognizing the validity of emotional struggles, partners can foster an environment of acceptance and support, where the journey to healing is undertaken hand in hand.

Cultivating Empathy: Our exploration has underscored the transformative power of empathy. By walking in each other's shoes and striving to understand the depth of emotional experiences, partners strengthen their emotional connection and create a safe haven for vulnerability.

The Power of Open Communication: We've emphasized the vital role of open communication in creating a relationship that thrives on mutual understanding. By sharing thoughts, fears, and aspirations openly, partners create a space where trust and emotional connection flourish.

Prioritizing Mental Well-Being: Mental well-being is a shared journey that requires equal dedication from both partners. Our journey has shown that supporting each other's mental health doesn't diminish the partnership but strengthens it, fostering resilience and growth.

A Path to the Future: As we conclude this exploration, remember that your journey as a couple is ongoing. Challenges will arise, but armed with the tools of open communication, empathy, and mutual support, you're equipped to navigate them with grace and strength.

A Call to Action: We encourage you to embrace the lessons learned and continue fostering a partnership that places mental well-being at its core.

Make a commitment to prioritize open conversations about mental health, actively seek understanding, and provide unwavering support to each other.

Thank You: Thank you for embarking on this journey with us, and for your dedication to nurturing a relationship that flourishes on empathy and shared growth. By prioritizing mental health awareness and support, you're creating a legacy of love, resilience, and emotional well-being that will shape your journey together for years to come.

With Warm Regards,

LAGANG PRINCEWILL

www.ingramcontent.com/pod-product-compliance
Lightning Source LLC
LaVergne TN
LVHW020455080526
838202LV00057B/5966